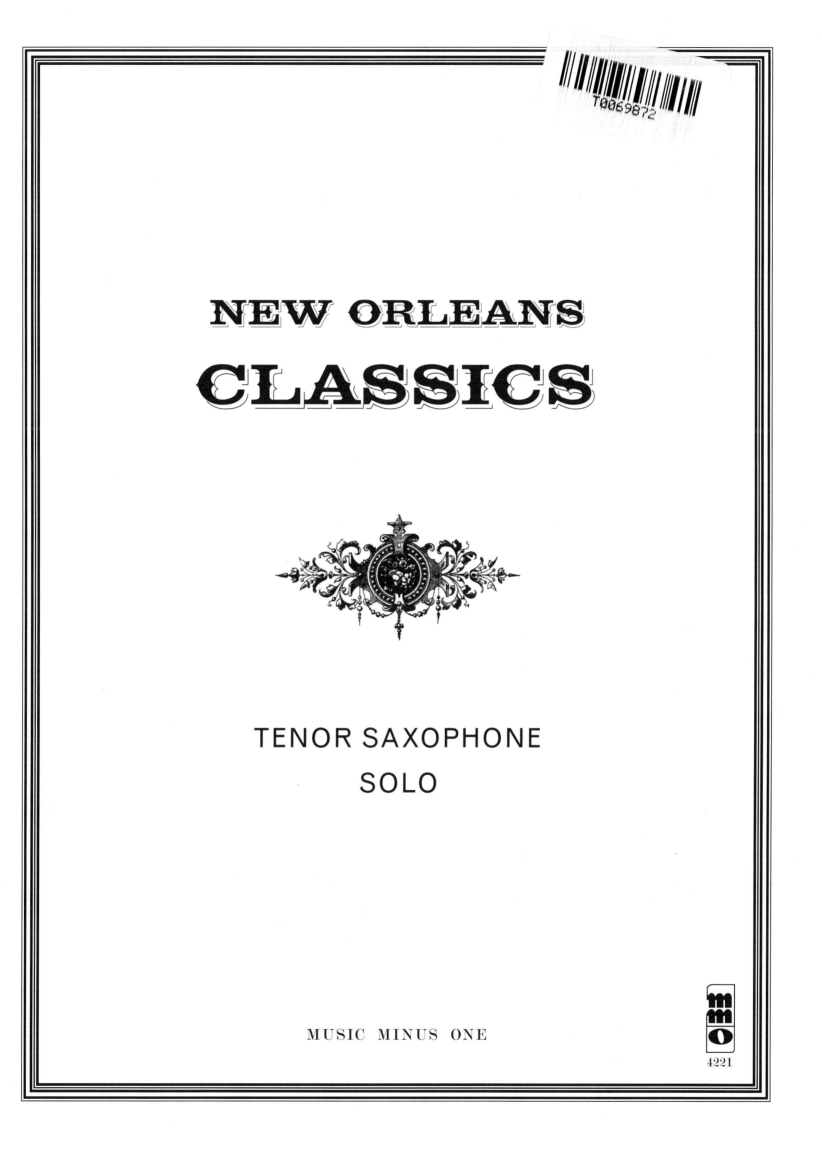

NEW ORLEANS
CLASSICS

TENOR SAXOPHONE
SOLO

MUSIC MINUS ONE

4221

SUGGESTIONS FOR USING THIS MMO EDITION

WE HAVE TRIED to create a product that will provide you an easy way to learn and perform these compositions with a full ensemble in the comfort of your own home. Because it involves a fixed accompaniment performance, there is an inherent lack of flexibility in tempo. The following MMO features and techniques will reduce these inflexibilities and help you maximize the effectiveness of the MMO practice and performance system:

We have observed generally accepted tempi, and always in the originally intended key, but some may wish to perform at a different tempo, or to slow down or speed up the accompaniment for practice purposes; or to alter the piece to a more comfortable key. We have included slow-tempo versions of the most up-tempo pieces on this album for practice and/or a slower interpretation. But for even more flexibility, you can purchase from MMO specialized CD players & recorders which allow variable speed while maintaining proper pitch, and vice versa. This is an indispensable tool for the serious musician and you may wish to look into purchasing this useful piece of equipment for full enjoyment of all your MMO editions.

We want to provide you with the most useful practice and performance accompaniments possible. If you have any suggestions for improving the MMO system, please feel free to contact us. You can reach us by e-mail at info@musicminusone.com.

CONTENTS

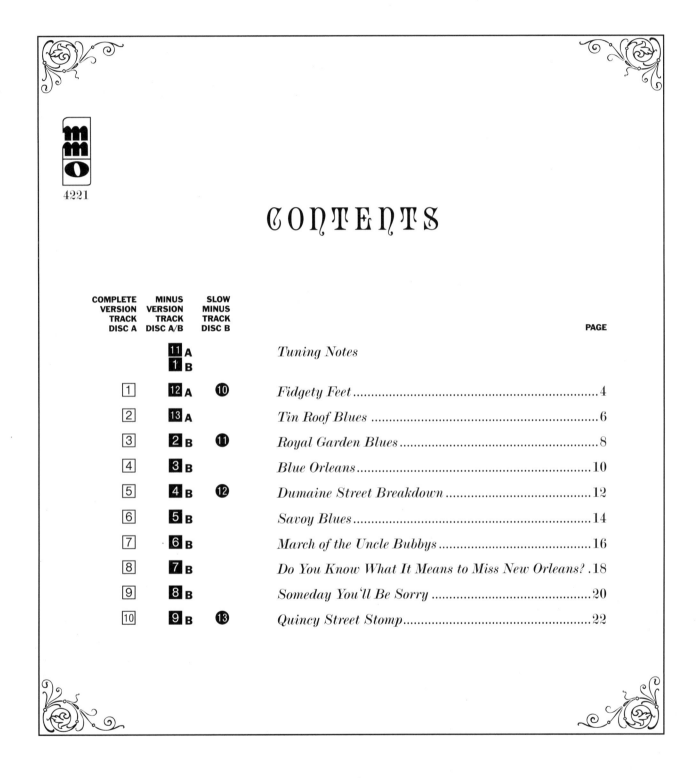

Tenor Saxophone in Bb

Fidgety Feet

Original Dixieland Jass Band

Tenor Saxophone in Bb

Tin Roof Blues

New Orleans Rhythm Kings

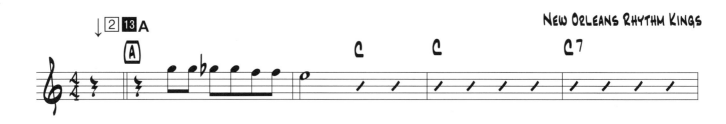

MMO 4221

Royal Garden Blues

Clarence & Spencer Williams

TENOR SAXOPHONE IN B♭

Blue Orleans

TIM LAUGHLIN

CLARINET SOLO

Tenor Saxophone in Bb

Dumaine Street Breakdown

Tim Laughlin

Tenor Saxophone in Bb

Savoy Blues

Edward "Kid" Ory

MMO 4221

TENOR SAXOPHONE IN Bb

March of the Uncle Bubbys

TIM LAUGHLIN

TROMBONE SOLO
32

TROMBONE-CLARINET DUET
16

ADD CORNET
16

DIXIELAND BAND ENSEMBLE

DRUMS

MMO 4221

TENOR SAXOPHONE IN Bb

Do You Know What It Means to Miss New Orleans?

EDDIE DELANGE
LOUIS ALTER

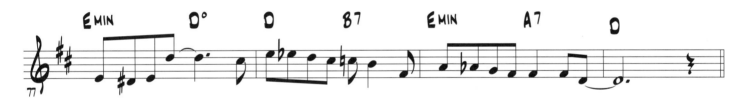

Tenor Saxophone in B♭

Someday You'll Be Sorry

TENOR SAXOPHONE IN Bb

Quincy Street Stomp

SIDNEY BECHET

MUSIC MINUS ONE
50 Executive Boulevard
Elmsford, New York 10523-1325
1.800.669.7464 (U.S.)/914.592.1188 (International)

www.musicminusone.com
e-mail: mmogroup@musicminusone.com

MMO 4221   Pub. No. 00253   Printed in Canada